AVISSON YOUNG ADULT SERIES

Yao Ming
Gentle Giant of Basketball

Richard Krawiec

Avisson Press Inc.
Greensboro

Copyright © 2004 by Richard Krawiec. All rights reserved. For information, contact Avisson Press Inc., P.O. Box 38816, Greensboro, NC 27438 USA.

ISBN 1-888105-63-1
First edition
Printed in the USA

Library of Congress Cataloging-in-Publication Data
Krawiec, Richard
  Yao Ming : gentle giant of basketball / Richard Krawiec. —1st ed.
    p. cm.— (Avisson young adult series)
  Summary: A biography of Yao Ming, the Chinese basketball player who is a star with the Houston Rockets.
  Includes bibliographical references and index.
  ISBN 1-888105-63-1
  1. Yao, Ming, 1980—Juvenile literature. 2. Basketball players—China—Biography—Juvenile literature. [1. Yao, Ming, 1980- 2.Basketball players.] I. Title. II. Series.

GV884.Y66K73 2003
796.323'092—dc22
[B]

2003059385

PICTURE CREDITS: All photographs including cover courtesy of AP / Wide World Photos

Table of Contents

Introduction 5
First Sighting 8
The Early Years 11
Television Heroes 18
The Europeans 21
Business and Basketball 26
International Competition 32
Growing Up 34
Getting Closer 37
Coming on Strong 43
On the World Stage 47
A New Champion 52
Risks and Hopes 62
Marketing Yao Ming 69
First Taste 75
Glimpses of Success 79
All Star Controversy 85
The New Racism? 88
A Tired Finish 95
Bibliography 105
Index 107

Introduction

The biggest sporting event in the USA is the National Football League's championship game, the Superbowl. Every January the two teams that have survived a grueling series of playoff games compete to claim the title as the world's best football team. An estimated 137 million television viewers watched in 2003 as Tampa played Oakland in SuperBowl XXXVII.

But the Superbowl is not just about football. It has become the premiere advertising event of the year, with companies unveiling their newest, and hopefully best, television commercials. The competition to produce the most memorable ad is just as intense as the competition on the football field.

In 2003, the ad that received the most lasting buzz, the ad that lodged in the memories of viewers for months afterwards, featured a very tall, thin Chinese man who enters a clothing store and asks a simple question to a short, brown-haired American girl who has the tough attitude of a hardened New York City dweller.

The man asks if he can cash a check.

"Yo," the girl says, slashing her thumb back at a sign that says No Checks Cashed.

The man looks down sheepishly at the name embroidered on his shirt and nods. "Yao," he says, as if correcting her.

"Yo," she says again, with a bit more disdain, a touch more anger.

"Yao," the man insists politely.

"Yo," the girl says, calling over a male employee, who responds, when the Chinese man asks him about cashing a check, with the same thumb pointing and abrupt call of "Yo."

"Yao," the man says, polite yet insistent.

Two customers, young men in baggy pants, recognize the man for who he is and exclaim, "Yo!"

"Yao," the man, frustrated, gives up.

It is this ad that signaled the arrival of Yao Ming as an American icon, a star, a popular force that would quickly become a part of our cultural consciousness. Long after memories of the Superbowl game itself, of individual plays, the final score, or even which teams competed, have faded from public memory, Americans will remember the polite, well-mannered, young man, with a kind of Jackie Chan humility, and his Yo-Yao confusion. The football game, the most popular sporting event in the United States, had been upstaged by a rookie basketball player from China.

First Sighting

The Nike company sent Terry Rhoads to China in 1994 to be their Director of Marketing for that country. He was the man responsible for convincing the Chinese people to buy Nike shoes. Why China? Well, their population is about 500% larger than the population of the United States. There are some 2.6 billion feet in China that the conpany wanted to see wearing Nike sneakers.

In 1997, Rhoads decided Nike should sponsor a team in the Chinese Basketball Association, a new league that had been formed only two years earlier. The CBA had not established itself yet as a quality basketball league, but it was officially supported by the Chinese government. Nike chose to sponsor the Shanghai Sharks. The Sharks were one of the weaker teams in the league, but Shanghai was a bustling, international city with a population of 14 million. The population numbers of their home city outweighed any concerns about the team's poor record. To make the Sharks even more enticing, they were owned by a television station. For a sports apparel manufacturer, TV translated to exposure.

For Nike, sponsoring the team offered the company a 'toehold' in a country that their analysts were predicting would soon be the largest, most lucrative market for basketball shoes, and related products, in the world.

What most people in the United States don't realize, is that the Chinese people are crazy about basketball. The NBA has been broadcasting games to China since 1989. Stylized, Pokemon-style drawings of NBA basketball players fill the wall-sized murals that surround Shanghai's public basketball courts. Sneakers associated with top NBA stars sell for upwards of $100, roughly one month's salary for many Chinese workers.

So sponsoring a team seemed like a good idea for Nike.

When the sponsorship deal was signed, a

party was organized to celebrate the partnership between the Sharks and the athletic shoe company. This would provide Rhoads, and other Nike representatives, an opportunity to get to know their Chinese counterparts, and also meet the Sharks' players.

As Rhoads told Cal Fussman, a writer for the online magazine *ESPNMAG.com*, "A few of us were there when in walked the team. Looked normal, guys around 6'4". Then this one kid comes in, baby-faced, who's about 7'3", kind of skinny ...Our jaws dropped, and then, of course, the skepticism came. Well, he's probably a stiff. But once he started hitting three-pointers, we thought —Whoa!"

A 7'3" center who could run, dribble, and shoot. Where had this kid come from?

The Early Years

Most Americans still hold the stereotyped notion that Chinese people are short. But there are areas in China where the people grow just as tall as people in the United States. Yao Ming comes from Shanghai, where the people do tend to be taller. His parents were also tall, and not just by Chinese standards. Even if they lived in the United States, Yao Ming's father and mother would tower over most of their peers.

Yao Zhi Yuan, Yao Ming's father, is 6'7" tall. Yao's mother, Fang Geng Di, is 6'3" tall. Both also happened to be basketball stars in their homeland. Yao Zhi Yuan played on a professional team in Shanghai. Fang Feng Di patrolled the center position and had served as captain for the Chinese National Women's team.

So it was no surprise that their child, born on Sept. 12, 1980, at an early age towered over his playmates. When Yao was only four, he was as tall as most children who were eight. By the time he reached the age of six, he had grown to the height of 4'9". Before he completed elementary school, he rose above nearly all of his teachers.

Given his height advantage, and the fact that his parents were skilled basketball players, it would seem natural that Yao would also excel at the sport. But at first that wasn't the case.

When Yao Ming was young, he wasn't particularly interested in basketball. Shanghai, where he grew up, was a vibrant, intellectual city, known for being in the forefront of scientific and educational pursuits. As a nine-year-old, Yao was more interested in science, in booklearning, than in running around on a basketball court.

His parents didn't want to force Yao to play basketball. They wanted him to make the decision for himself. Still, they enrolled him at the Youth Sports School.

At first, Yao's height advantage made no difference. He was in such bad physical shape, that running up and down the court a mere two times left him exhausted. Despite his height, he wasn't a muscular person. In fact, he was extremely skinny, weak, and uncoordinated. Smaller children regularly knocked Yao around, and beat him out of rebounds. They laughed at his slight frame, his thin arms, and called him 'chopsticks'.

Yao's parents encouraged their son not to get discouraged, not to give up. His coach explained that it took time to learn how to play basketball, to be patient with himself. Work at small improvements, his coach counseled. Get better one step at a time.

His mother and father taught their son what they knew about the game, in particular, how to play the center position. Basketball, however, is more than just a series of individual skills to be mastered. When a game is being played well by a team, there's a co-ordinated ebb and flow of motion back and forth down the court, with five people working together as one organism. His father took the time to explain the intricacies, the subtleties of the sport; a team game where individual skills meshed in a collective effort. Soon Yao Ming began to understand the beauty and grace of basketball. The more he understood, the more Ming learned to love the game.

When he was ten, and playing in his first organized children's league, Yao Ming's mother cooked him special treats before the game, so that he would look forward to game day. His father bought him small presents for every basket he made as a way to encourage his effort. His coach continued to tell Yao Ming to be patient, to look for improvement one step at a time.

This combination of encouragement and teaching had a positive effect on Yao. It helped him learn how to persevere. It taught him not to give up on himself. Soon, Yao began to develop more confidence.

In the long run, Yao's early failure probably helped him build character, too. He learned to be humble about his accomplishments, to appreciate whatever small successes he achieved.

For three years, Yao was trained and nurtured. By the time he turned twelve, he really loved basketball. There was no question that he was now serious about wanting to develop as a player. He was sent to a Shanghai sports academy, a preparatory school for young athletes. It is a place where children who are serious about developing their athletic skills would live away from home, sharing dorm rooms with other young children, and spend their days alternately attending classes and learning how to play their chosen sport.

This may seem somewhat strange to people living in the United States, where most children live at home at least until they finish high school.

But sports schools like the one Yao enrolled in when he was twelve are common throughout the world. In Russia, talented ice skaters are identified at an early age and moved away from their homes to enter sports academies. In Canada, hockey schools are a way of life for adolescent boys who dream of one day playing professionally in the National Hockey League.

Even in the United States, athletes often leave their families to train. Gymnasts and figure skaters frequently move in with their coaches, often when they're still in elementary school, so they have more time to spend on developing their talent. Sports academies are becoming more common with youth soccer players, too, who increasingly live away from home by the time they're teenagers.

In this country, many high-school-aged basketball players enroll in private academies where, although they attend classes, they are equally focused on developing their basketball skills, training for college and professional careers. Tracy McGrady, the all-star forward for the Orlando Magic, is just one example of a player who followed this route.

The experience of being at a sports academy was a good one for Yao Ming. When he turned fourteen, he was selected to be a member of the Shanghai Oriental Sharks, a youth team similar to an AAU(Amateur Athletic Union) team in the United States.

Yao Ming was developing into a good, young Chinese basketball player. Maybe one day he would achieve the same success on China's National team as his mother had.

But he soon learned there was more to basketball than what he'd seen in his homeland.

Yao Ming's basketball knowledge, and his personal horizons, were expanded by what he witnessed on TV.

Television Heroes

Just as Nike was moving into China, the NBA began broadcasting some of their games to Yao Ming's country. Ironically, the team Yao favored, was the one that would ultimately draft him as their #1 pick — the Houston Rockets. At that time, in the mid 1990s, Houston was led by Hall-of-Fame center Hakeem Olajuwon, another foreign-born player who had had great success in the United States.

In the 1990s, Hakeem Olajuwon was a different type of player than most centers in the NBA. Back then, the center was generally considered to be a power player. Most NBA centers were big, strong, but not particularly mobile. Their job was to use their size to muscle into the basket for dunks and putbacks, and to pull down rebounds. In essence, by virtue of their bulk, they were expected to take up space in the middle of the lane.

Gentle Giant of Basketball

But Olajuwon was undersized compared to most of his competition. He was only 6'9" tall, and he wasn't bulky. He was athletic in the way you expect a soccer player to be athletic, quick and fluid in his movements. In fact, he had grown up playing soccer in his native Nigeria. He didn't begin playing basketball until he reached high school.

Unable to get by on brute strength, Olajuwon used the skills he possessed - grace, athleticism, speed. He could outrun most opposing centers, could leap like a small forward, and sink a medium-range jump shot. He was one of the first of what would come to be the new breed of mobile, athletic big men.

For Yao Ming, watching Olajuwon gave him confidence. He saw someone playing his position, playing it at the highest level of competition, in a manner similar to how Yao's physical qualities would allow him to play. Yao realized that, like Olajuwon, he could use his speed to get up and down the court. Like Olajuwon, he could stay outside the lane, and use his height to shoot jump shots over the smaller defenders who played away from the basket.

For all of the training he had received, in an odd way it was television that brought to Yao Ming a true sense of what he might become as a basketball player. It was't just Hakeem Olajuwon that captured his interest, either. There was another center whose play was even more influential for the young Chinese star. This center didn't play in the United States, but he was clearly the most dominant big man in the rest of the world.

The Europeans

Growing up in the United States, it's easy to overlook what is happening in the rest of the world. This country is separated from most of the globe not just by two oceans, but by a media that often acts as if nothing of importance ever happens beyond our own borders. This is true in sports, just as much as it is true in politics. Often citizens of this country are ill-informed about sports competitions, and athletes, in other parts of the world.

In the United States, we consider our sports championship games to be the world championships. The NBA, the NFL, Major League Baseball - we consider the team that wins these championships to be the best in the world. We even call the baseball championship the World Series.

Yao Ming

It might well be true that our athletic teams are the best in the world. But the down side of this provincialism is that we often overlook talented athletes from other countries who play sports that we consider to be 'American'. The only time we recognize that other countries might be able to compete at the same level as our players, is every four years when we play in the Olympics.

Yao Ming grew up in a country that had more exposure to European and Asian sporting events than to sports competitions that occurred in the United States. He grew up watching European League basketball games on television. Although, as a whole, the basketball played in Europe wasn't as strong as that played in the NBA, there were many gifted players in that league.

So it was no surprise that Yao Ming's style of play was influenced by a man that even NBA scouts considered to be one of the best centers to ever play the game of basketball.

The man was Arvydas Sabonis. As Yao Ming was developing his skills in the 1990s, looking for

Gentle Giant of Basketball

a way to use his particular talents within the context of the game he loved, he found his greatest role model in a 7'3" center from Lithuania who was playing in Spain.

In the 1980s, Sabonis came to the attention of basketball fans when he played on the Soviet National teams. He wowed everyone who saw him, even American scouts. At 7'3" he was taller than most centers, and there was plenty of muscle on his big-boned frame.

But what was surprising about Sabonis was the high level of skills he brought to his game. He didn't just set up down low and overpower his opponents. He could hit outside jumpshots from as far away as 3-point range, although there was no three-point shot at that time. If he got the ball in the open court, he was able to dribble away from defenders and move it towards the basket. What made him particularly unique for a center, was his ability to pass the ball. He could thread the needle through traffic as well as any point guard. Many scouts considered him to be the best passing center they had ever seen play the game — anywhere, even in the NBA.

Yao Ming

When Ming watched Sabonis play on television in the mid-1990s, he knew that's how he wanted to play the game. He wanted to be a complete player, someone who could shoot, dribble, pass, as well as pull down rebounds and block shots. He wanted his game to be compared to that of Sabonis, because Sabonis' play brought out the grace and beauty of team play that Yao Ming had come to love.

As an impressionable teenager who was struggling to figure out how to use the physical tools he was born with in basketball, Yao Ming discovered two role models who could help him use his talents. Two centers he could pattern his game after.

Hakeem Olajuwon, the graceful center for the Houston Rockets who relied on his speed and agility to run the court and move around slower opposing players.

And Arvydas Sabonis, the big Lithuanian who used his intelligence and fine touch to throw pinpoint passes to his teammates or hit outside jump shots.

These two men showed Yao Ming how it was

possible for a center to dominate a game without being simply a big, bulky presence close to the basket. They showed Yao that dribbling, passing, shooting, and speedy footwork were skills he could use, not just for his own glory, but to help his team win.

In watching these two men play, Yao discovered how he could be himself.

Business and Basketball

When the Olympic Games were held in Atlanta in 1996, the Chinese team still wasn't ready for top international competition. Although the team featured two seven-footers who would go on to play in the NBA, Wang Zhi Zhi and Menk Bateer, they finished 8th in Olympic competition.

That low finish belied the popularity of the game in China. The Chinese Basketball Association was officially up and running, and one of the teams, the Shanghai Sharks, had just signed a scrawny sixteen year old, who was already close to seven feet tall, to play for them in the 1997-98 season.

That skinny sixteen-year-old was Yao Ming, who shocked the Nike executives with his height and game.

Business and basketball combined that year to begin the journey that would make Yao Ming an international marketing and basketball star. Sometimes it's unclear which came first — the marketing, or the basketball. Without the latter, though, the former would never happen.

Recognizing a potential star in the making, Nike invited Ming to attend a summer basketball camp that the sneaker-maker was running in Paris that summer of 1997. Some two hundred teenaged basketball players from all over Europe attended the camp. Although the competition was stiff, this was the first time that Yao was one of the older players. In China, he always played against people who were older, and more experienced.

In Paris, he only had to compete against his peers.

Not only did he compete, but he more than held his own. He stunned the camp leaders by his dominant play.

According to Cal Fussman, one of those in attendance at the Paris camp, Del Harris, who was at that time coaching the Los Angeles Lakers, told everyone: "I gotta get a picture with this kid because one day he's going to have a real impact in the NBA."

Yao Ming was no longer an oddity, a tall skinny freak from China. He had established himself as a player, someone to watch for the future.

And Nike, a company known for its business savvy, recognized the advantage in helping Ming develop. There was that whole China market to keep in mind, those 2.6 billion feet. So after Paris, Nike negotiated with the Chinese government and received permission for Yao Ming to leave his homeland and spend the summer in the United States, where the level of play, and coaching, would spur Yao's development.

It was a win-win-win situation. One of China's elite young players would essentially receive two months of free training, then return to his homeland better able to lead China in international competition. Yao Ming would certainly progress faster under the guidance of U.S. coaches, and by having to compete against elite teenaged athletes. Nike was also establishing a good relationship with a player who could possibly become a major international figure in the sports, and marketing, scene.

Yao Ming was brought to the United States and added to the roster of an elite American AAU(Amateur Athletic Union) team. He spent two months learning the intricacies of the American version of basketball.

From there, he attended the All America Camp in Indianapolis. At that camp, two hundred of the best teenaged players in the United States were gathered to perform in drills and scrimmages. The All America camp offers an opportunity for college recruiters to scrutinize the best young high school players in the United States, and, in Yao Ming's case, from China. The recruiters and camp staff grade the players in all aspects of the game — dribbling, shooting, passing, rebounding, etc.

Yao was placed in a group of forty kids who played the center position. At the end of camp, when the final grades were announced, Yao Ming had the second highest score among the forty centers in attendance.

His stock wasn't just rising. It had exploded.

Success breeds opportunity. In this case, Ming's showing at the All America camp earned him an invitation to Santa Barbara, California, where he would work as a counselor at a youth basketball camp run by Nike's most prominent salesman, Michael Jordan, by consensus the greatest basketball player in the world.

For the counselors, the highlight of the camp experience came when their workday was finished. Every night they would scrimmage each other. Jordan himself would come to the court to scrimmage with the teenagers.

As Rhoads told Fussman: "I remember Michael coming downcourt one game, sinking a three-pointer, and teasing Yao. You know, 'Can you do that?' So Yao launches a three-pointer and hits, and Michael's saying, "Wow! The big guy can shoot!"

It was an exciting moment for Yao Ming. And for Nike.

From that point on, it was a foregone conclusion that Yao Ming would one day wind up in the NBA. It was clear he had the athletic gifts needed to succeed in basketball. And as Bill Duffy, Yao's first agent, recognized, this wasn't just a basketball matter, either. Duffy felt Yao's marketing potential was so great there was no way to understand how huge a phenomenon the kid might become.

International Competition

Success in any sport is fifty percent physical, fifty percent mental. Having confidence in one's ability to perform in a game situation is just as important as having the physical skills necessary to perform. Without self confidence, skills mean little.

Yao Ming's experience in the United States in the summer of 1997 helped him develop his game. More importantly, it proved to him that he was capable of not just competing against the best young players in the world, but of excelling against them. He returned from the United States as a player to watch.

He returned ready for the next challenge.

But Yao's improved skill and confidence didn't result in immediate success on the court for his Chinese team, the Shanghai Sharks.

Although he certainly understood the game

better, Ming was still physically weak. His muscle structure hadn't developed yet. As a skinny seventeen-year-old, Yao Ming had to compete against older, stronger, more experienced players. He was regularly knocked all over the court. The Shanghai Sharks finished 8th in the 12-team Chinese Basketball Association in the 1997-1998 season.

Disappointed, but not discouraged, Yao Ming joined the Chinese National Junior Team and began preparations to play at the Asian Basketball Confederation Tournament, which would be held in Calcutta, India the summer of 1998.

Ming led the Chinese Junior Men's team to a first place finish. In the championship game against Qatar, Ming blocked 17 shots. It was an achievement he would often cite years later as one of his greatest performances. For his play, Yao Ming was named the MVP of the tournament.

Growing Up

Ming continued to play for China's Junior Men's teams in competitions throughout Asia that summer. He learned a lot. He was really beginning to understand the importance of playing defense, how a blocked shot was just as important as a basket made. He understood that personal statistics were only important if they helped your team win, and that you could help your team win without dominating the score sheet. He was improving, one step at a time.

And he was growing physically. As he approached his 18th birthday, his body started to fill out. His legs, in particular, grew bulkier, more muscular, strong enough now for him to hold his position in the low post. During the season, CBA opponents found out it was no longer an easy task to move Ming away from the basket.

He had worked hard in the preseason to

develop a more rounded, balanced game. The practice time paid off. Ming scored 25 points per game, and pulled down 15 rebounds for the Sharks. More importantly, the Shanghai Sharks improved. The team rose to a respectable 4th place finish in the CBA.

After the CBA season, he was promoted to China's National Men's team, where he would be competing in tournaments throughout the summer of 1999.

This would be the highest level of competition Yao Ming had ever played. He was put on a front line with future NBA players Wang Zhi Zhi and Menk Bateer. The three of them were dubbed the 'Walking Great Wall' of China.

But Yao Ming was no longer the star of a team, only one of many important players. Still, at the Asian Basketball Confederation Championship Games for Men, which were held in Fukuoka, Japan, Yao Ming averaged 12 points and 7 rebounds per game.

More important than his scoring was his defensive presence. Ming was active on the defensive end, blocking or altering shots, making it difficult for opposing players to even get their shots off near the basket.

China easily stormed through the competition to win the Championship.

The Chinese team may have been feeling too confident about their easy victory at the ABC games. Yao Ming and his teammates were soon given a reality check when they entered the tougher Fila Junior World Championships.

For their first game of the tournament, they were matched against the United States. The US team utterly destroyed the Chinese team, winning 119-59. It was a crushing, humiliating loss.

China never recovered. They won only one game in that tournament before hanging their heads and slinking home.

Getting Closer

In the 1999-2000 CBA season, Yao and the Shanghai Sharks both progressed another level. Yao's game was more polished, and the Sharks finished two slots higher in the CBA, in second place. They still trailed the Bayi Rockets in the standings, and although Ming and company might've had hopes they were ready for that final step, the truth is, they weren't there yet.

With Wang Zhi Zhi dominating, the Rockets swept three straight games from the Sharks to win the league championship again. It was one more lesson for Yao about success coming one small step at a time.

That season was an important, if somewhat unsettling one for the Chinese Basketball Association. Several of their players were being looked at closely by the NBA. The Dallas Mavericks were desperately trying to sign Wang Zhi Zhi, whom they had drafted in the second round in the June 1999 entry draft. There were whispers that it was time for Yao Ming to make himself available for the NBA draft. And the Chinese National team, which featured players from the CBA, had to prepare for the summer Olympics, which would be held in Australia.

China felt pressure, not just because the eyes of the Western World would be taking a close look at their basketball players, but because they were the only Asian country to enter a basketball team in Olympic competition. So they were competing for regional, as well as national, pride.

Along with Wang Zhi Zhi and Menk Bateer, Yao Ming formed a frontline of seven footers. Although few U.S. fans knew anything about the three players because Chinese basketball was not featured on American television, NBA scouts and representatives from athletic-wear companies were excited at their prospects should the Chinese players perform well.

This excitement was diluted with caution. No one really gave China much of a chance to actually win an Olympic medal. The Chinese Basketball Association was considered to be the equivalent to Division II (college) basketball in the United States. Even good Division II teams were not capable of competing with top basketball colleges like Duke, Kentucky, UCLA, North Carolina, or Arizona. Also, it was rare for a Division II *player* to make it to the NBA.

As luck would have it, China's first game was against a U.S. Dream Team composed of NBA (pro) all-stars.

In the first quarter, Yao Ming came out strong. He blocked shots by Vince Carter and Gary Payton. China actually led early, by scores of 13-7 then 17-16.

At that point, the U.S. team woke up. They turned it on, and cruised to a 47 point victory, 119-72.

Yao Ming scored only 5 points and grabbed just 3 rebounds, but back home his countrymen appreciated the effort Yao put out, the fact that he was willing to battle hard, and not back down.

When the tournament was over, Chinese citizens could raise their heads in pride to learn that Yao Ming had finished 2nd in blocked shots, and 6th in rebounding for the tournament.

Yao Ming

The whispers became louder. Surely, Yao was good enough to turn pro. Yes, he would need to work on his game, but his potential was at least as high as that of several of the American high school players, players like Eddie Curry and Tyson Chandler, who were rumored to be putting their names in for the NBA draft. Wasn't Yao as good as those two young players?

But decisions in China aren't as simple as they are in the United States. It's not just a matter of a teenager announcing he will make himself available for the NBA draft. There were two major obstacles on Ming's path to professional basketball.

The Shanghai Sharks had been steadily improving as Yao improved, and seemed on the verge of winning a championship. They were also now selling out their games. As a government-run league, with revenues being returned to the Chinese government, the possibility of lost revenue was not appealing. So, the government would have to give Yao Ming permission to leave the team, and they seemed reluctant to do so.

Then there was the larger issue of the Chinese

government's willingness to let Yao leave the country. Unlike in the United States, Chinese citizens don't have the right to make all decisions about their own lives. The level of governmental control extends to almosr every aspect of a person's life.

For example, Yao Ming, like almost all children in China, is an only child because the government forbids parents from having more than one child, a measure to decrease the huge population.

If Yao Ming were to be allowed to enter the NBA draft, the Chinese government would have to be appeased. Payments and contracts would have to be made, and agreements signed that would allow Yao to play for China's national team during the NBA off-season. Ming's Chinese team, the Shanghai Sharks, would have to be appeased, too. There were a whole slew of considerations.

But those in the United States who wanted to see a Chinese star play in this country — agents, marketers, the NBA — felt they had a major trump card they could play.

Yao Ming

China desperately wanted to host the 2008 Summer Olympics. The American sports and marketing executives who wanted to see Yao Ming play in this county might be able to insure that China would win their bid — if the Chinese government allowed Yao Ming to play in the NBA.

Coming on Strong

If all the public posturing and behind-the-scenes negotiating bothered Yao Ming, he certainly didn't show it. In the 2000-2001 basketball season, Ming played the best basketball of his life.

His defensive positioning had improved, and he displayed an increased variety of shots, including dunks - which Yao had picked up from his exposure to the American game.

In the collectivist culture of China, the emphasis was on team, the group, over the individual. Dunks were frowned upon. They seemed to draw attention to the player doing the dunking.

But at the camps he'd attended, Yao had been told that, like it or not, he would have to show he could dunk to play center in the NBA.

In the 2000-2001 season, Yao increased his

scoring to average 27 points per game. Many of those points came on dunks, as if to show NBA scouts he could play an American-style game, too.

He also improved his defense, as was reflected by pulling down 19.4 rebounds per game — best in the CBA — and averaging 5.5 blocks.

For the first time in his young career, Yao Ming was selected for the CBA all-star game. As if that weren't enough, to cap his personal success, he won the league MVP award.

Still, personal statistics only matter if they help your team win.

Once more, the Shanghai Sharks faced the Bayi Rockets in the CBA championships series.

Once again, the Rockets won. Although the Sharks weren't swept this time, they were handily defeated by the Rockets, 3 games to 1.

Still, American basketball aficionados began to discuss in earnest whether Yao Ming was ready to make the next step up; to enter his name in the NBA draft. China seemed willing to consider the possibility. At least initially they were willing to listen.

But as reported in *Sports Illustrated online*, American greed sabotaged negotiations.

Agent Frank Duffy had been working with Ming's family for two years. But with Yao's sudden ascendancy, super agent David Falk, one of the most powerful sports agents in the United States, swooped in and tried to arrange, through the Shanghai Sharks, for Yao Ming to be represented by Falk's SFX Sports Group.

A third agent, Michael Coyne, also became involved in the mess. He had previously signed a contract with the Sharks that allowed him to take a hefty percentage of any money Ming might earn from the NBA through June, 2000.

Frank Duffy sent letters to Billy Hunter, the Executive Director of the NBA Players Union, and NBA Commissioner David Stern, in which Duffy threatened to file a lawsuit to protect his interests in Ming.

The public bickering over the rights to Yao Ming was ugly and disturbing to the Chinese government; it decided not to release Yao Ming to play in the NBA. The Shanghai Sharks held a press conference to announce that Yao Ming would focus his attention solely on preparing to play for the Chinese National team in the upcoming summer international basketball tournaments.

Without a word of protest or complaint, Ming switched his attention from the NBA draft to his role as a member of the Chinese National Team. First up, the East Asian Games, held in Japan that year.

On the World Stage

In the United States most people, when they think about competitive basketball, think of the NBA, college hoops, and the Olympics.

Increasingly, with the influx of foreign-born players in the NBA, more US citizens are learning to recognize that the basketball world is larger than they had realized.

Still, most Americans have little knowledge of global basketball competition.

For Yao Ming, the CBA season was followed by an even busier series of tournaments over the summer months.

First up were the Asian Games, held in Japan that year.

The Asian Games were begun after World War II, at India's suggestion. They were seen as a way to promote intercultural knowledge and friendship among the countries in Asia, outside of European influence.

At the first games, held in New Delhi in 1951, eleven countries, including Japan, participated. The games settled into a schedule where they were held every 4 years, in-between the Olympic years. Representatives from each country compete in judged events that include not only sports but architecture, painting, sculpture, music, and traditional arts. Participating countries now include, among others, Afghanistan, Lebanon, Palestine, Turkemenistan, Indonesia, and Australia.

China performed well, finishing second after losing to Australia, 105-93, in the championship game.

From there, they moved on to play in the Pan Asian games. This time China won all 8 games to earn the championship. Ming added another MVP trophy to his display case.

Next up were the Universiade Games, hosted that summer by Beijing. Ming would be playing at home.

Gentle Giant of Basketball

The Universiade Games are so-named because they are similar to the Olympics, but the competitors are students from around the world. They developed out of the World Student Games, which were first held in 1923 in Paris. These games, and the ones in succeeding years, featured student athletes from Europe. Like the Olympics, a different country hosted them each year.

After World War II, the games split into two separate competitions, East and West, mimicking the lines of the Cold War Alliances. They were still seen as a European competition. In the 1953 games, held in Italy, the United States only sent 3 athletes to compete.

The first joint games between East and West were held in 1957, hosted by the city that originally hosted the Student Games — Paris.

The first official 'Universiade Games' were held in 1959, in Turin, Italy, under the auspices of the International University Sports Federation.

Initially the Winter Universiade Games were

held in odd numbered years and the Summer in even numbered years.

Today, they are a biannual event, with Winter and Summer games held in the same year, every other year.

Although the Universiade Games receive scant media attention in the United States, they are popular worldwide and attract many of the best international student athletes. Tens of thousands of spectators attend from all over the globe to watch the students perform.

In the Summer of 2001, the team representing the United States in basketball at the Universiade games, was led by two players from the University of Maryland, the college that won the NCAA title. Those players were NBA first round draft picks, center Lonnie Baxter and guard Juan Dixon, who also won the Naismith Award as the best college basketball player in the U.S. during the 2001-2002 season.

For the semi-finals, China had to face the U.S. team. The U.S. had won 46 straight games in competition at the Universiades.

In the most stunning upset of the

tournament, China won the game by 1 point, 83-82. Yao Ming scored 12 points in the victory.

Perhaps the team was too elated by their victory, or emotionally drained from having pulled an upset over the U.S. team. Whatever the reason, they suffered a massive letdown in the championship game. Yugoslavia trounced China by forty points, 101-61.

It was back to China for the 2001-2002 season. A season that would change the course of Yao Ming's future.

A New Champion

Expectations were high for Yao Ming and the Shanghai Sharks as the 2001-2002 Chinese Basketball Association season began. The Sharks, to improve their chances at a title run, had added two American players, one of them Lloyd, 'Sweat Pea' Daniels, a playground legend who had handled a few brief stints in the NBA.

The Americans added a certain swagger, a toughness to the Chinese team. Yao remembers that the first thing they wanted to learn was how to 'trash talk' in Chinese.

And everyone was looking for big improvement from Yao, who would soon turn twenty-two. He looked stronger physically - he was up to 7'5" tall, and 295 pounds. With all the international competition he'd experienced, expectations were high that this would be the season Ming would finally dominate the competition.

Yao didn't disappoint. He averaged 29.7 points, 18.5 rebounds, and 4.8 blocks per game. The Sharks lost only 1 game, finishing the season with a 23-1 record. They swept through the first two rounds of the CBA playoffs and entered the Championship series to find themselves facing a familiar foe: the Bayi Rockets.

But these weren't exactly the same Rockets who had handily defeated the Sharks in each of the last two years. Star center Wang Zhi Zhi, who had been drafted in the 2nd round in 1999 by the Dallas Mavericks, had finally been allowed by the Chinese government to go play in the NBA. He was overseas now, trying to help Dallas earn a playoff berth.

And these weren't even the same Sharks that had stormed through the CBA during the season. To strengthen their chance at a title, a third American, David Benoit, a swing man who had years of experience playing in tough playoff series during the 1990s as a member of the Utah

Yao Ming

Yao, as first round draft pick for the Houston Rockets, is presented a Rockets jersey by new teammates Steve Francis, center, and Cuttino Mobley during a pre-game ceremony in Houston, October 2002.

Jazz, was signed to give Shanghai an added advantage.

Still, it was close. The series went to the final game, with the Sharks winning the CBA Championship, 3 games to 2. Unquestionably the best player on the court throughout the series was Yao Ming. He improved on his already stunning regular season success by averaging 41 points and 21 rebounds per game.

His performance silenced all but the most

hardcore critics. Most basketball analysts now believed Yao Ming was ready for the NBA. Negotiations between the Chinese government and the NBA began in earnest. The Americans wanted Yao to enter the June NBA draft.

As talk of Yao's availability for the draft became more heated, rumors started to float around NBA circles. Ming might be available if he could pick his city, the rumor-mongers claimed. He wanted to play in San Francisco, Chicago, or New York — cities with large Chinatown sections, where he could be around others who spoke his language and cooked food the way he preferred.

The rumors were false. Yao Ming, and China, were making no such demands. To begin with, a Chinatown full of immigrants, many of whom had fled the repressive regime in mainland China, would not necessarily be attractive to a government wanting to control how Yao Ming viewed his homeland.

On the other hand, it was a well-known fact that Yao Ming's favorite restaurant in Shanghai was Tony Roma's, an American steak house.

Yao Ming

As fate would have it, Houston won the draft lottery. Houston had the 8th largest Asian population of any U.S. city. Nearly 5% of their population was Asian, primarily Chinese. As a smaller city, the Houston media was less critical, more kind to its athletes than one might find in larger, more cynical places.

For Yao Ming, what made Houston particularly enticing was the fact that the Rockets were coached by Rudy Tomjanovich. Rudy T. had also coached the Rockets when Hakeem Olajuwon, a foreign-born center with non-traditional skills, played for Houston. The Rockets had won two world championships under Rudy T's leadership.

This, Yao Ming thought, might be an ideal situation for him.

But there were two problems with this scenario.

There was no guarantee that Yao Ming would be the #1 draft pick. There were many excellent players in the 2002 draft, including Duke University's senior guard, and player of the year,

Gentle Giant of Basketball

Jay Williams, and high school standout Amare Stoudamire.

Also, and potentially more problematic, Ming's release to the NBA had not been worked out with the Chinese government.

This was turning out to be a bigger problem than once thought. Despite the previous year's bickering between agents, China had seemed willing to work out a deal for Yao's release.

Then the Dallas Mavericks got into the act.

China had requested that Wang Zhi Zhi return home to play for the Chinese National team.

But Dallas didn't jump to comply. And neither did Zhi Zhi.

The Chinese government was miffed. What if Yao Ming were released to play in the United States, then didn't honor his commitment to the Chinese National Team? The thought of playing in international competition without two of their stars seemed incomprehensible to the Chinese Government.

If they released Yao Ming to the NBA, what guarantees did they have that the Houston

Rockets would not renege on their agreement, like Dallas had with Wang Zhi Zhi?

The Houston Rockets did everything they could to reassure the Chinese government that their intentions were honorable. The NBA, Nike, other U.S. marketing concerns all worked hard to insure Yao's availability for the NBA draft.

Still, the Chinese government was reluctant.

Yao Ming was powerless to do anything about the political negotiations. He had no role to play in negotiating his release from China. So he did the only thing he could.

He joined the Chinese national team to prepare for the World Basketball Championships being held in Indianapolis that year.

He was invited to attend a pre-draft workout in Chicago that summer, run by former NBA coach P.J. Carlessimo. No one would've blamed Yao Ming had he chosen to miss the camp, since he had to travel all the way from China. But it was a sign of his determination and character that he didn't take the easy way out.

At the camp, NBA scouts and coaches ran Ming, and two other players, through drills designed to measure everything from their leaping, shooting, dribbling, and rebounding ability, to their stamina and speed. The players also scrimmaged each other, so the NBA observers could get a feel for how they might react in a game situation.

China had not allowed Yao Ming any time to prepare for the tryout. As expected, Ming was tired. He did show a good shooting touch, nice footwork, and passing skills, but his defense

Yao towers over the crowd after attending a speech by Chinese President Jiang Zemin at the George Bush Presidential Library Center, Texas A & M University.

wasn't as strong as anticipated. His performance left many scouts uncertain, although not those from the Houston Rockets. The Rockets' personnel picked up on one thing others might have missed - Yao's great desire to succeed.

When the tryout camp was over, Ming released a statement that was published on NBA.com. His words impressed many for what they showed about his character. It wasn't just what he said — anyone can mouth the proper words of thanks. It was the sincerity that came through, and even the sense of humor, that made the pros take notice.

"I am humbled and grateful for the unforgettable experience the past few days. I would like first to thank the NBA for hosting this event in the great city of Chicago. The superb organization demonstrates a level of professionalism that I truly admire.

"I would also like to express my sincere gratitude to all NBA teams for showing interest in me. I am honored by your presence. And I hope I have not disappointed you with my performance today. Proper credit is also due to the members of the media...your resourcefulness and work ethic are something I think we players should emulate...I look forward to taking each and every one of you to dinner sometime in the future. But the check is on you if your reporting makes me look bad.

"Last but certainly not least, I owe the greatest debt of gratitude to the fans of basketball everywhere. You gave me the greatest job on Earth. And I promise to repay your trust by respecting the game, and by challenging myself to be the best that I can be."

As the draft approached, Houston frantically tried to work out a deal with the Chinese government. They were convinced Yao Ming was the player they wanted.

But there were still doubters who questioned whether or not Yao deserved to be the #1 pick.

Risks and Hopes

The number of basketball 'experts' who doubted that Yao Ming deserved to be the #1 pick in the NBA draft was dwindling, though it had not disappeared.

The draft is not an exact science. People forget that the greatest basketball player of all time, Michael Jordan, was picked third the year he entered the NBA. The Number One pick that year? Sam Bowie.

Who is Bowie, you might ask? That's the point.

Kobe Bryant went 8th in the draft when he entered out of high school. Although he struggled in his early years, he has certainly gone on to prove he is a superstar.

But for every Kobe Bryant there's a Dewayne Stevenson.

Gentle Giant of Basketball

For a while, after Hakeem Olajuwon came out of Africa to become a star, NBA scouts were convinced Africa would be fertile territory for the next generation of NBA superstars, especially dominating big men.

While Dikembe Mutumbo did achieve stardom, 7'7" Manute Bol became no better than a super-tall curiosity item, better suited for Ripley's Believe it or Not than the NBA Hall of Fame. Then there with others, like Yinka Dare, who quickly faded into obscurity.

So there were still a number of questions about whether a player from China could seriously compete in the United States. The level of competition, the lack of training, certainly, these critics argued, would prevent Yao Ming from ever becoming a solid player.

In May, 2002, Bill Simons wrote for *ESPN.com*, "Years from now, we will remember 'Yao Ming over Jay Williams' the same way we remember 'Bowie over Jordan'... This is a disaster waiting to happen. Repeat: This is a disaster waiting to happen."

But there were others who felt Ming, and

Yao Ming

Houston Rockets Teammate Glenn Rice congratulates Yao during the closing minutes of their victory over the Indiana Pacers on December 18, 2002. Yao led the Rockets with 29 points.

other Chinese players, would be more likely to make the transition to the NBA.

Donnie Nelson, Assistant Coach of the Dallas Mavericks, in a June 6, 2002 article written by

Gentle Giant of Basketball

Michael Murphy for *Houstonchronicle.com* pointed out that in Africa, "There is virtually no infrastructure at all...the guys who make it out of there are either flat-out lucky, or they're mistakes."

By contrast, China, and the other Asian countries, have a solid developmental training program. "They have national programs that are reliable...a professional system...a developmental system for their youth."

Attorney and agent Michael Coyne pointed out, "China has more of a regional club system...The Sharks get everybody in their region. They advertise all over China for 8-year-olds, and they ship them up to their training center...And they have junior teams...If you see an 8-year-old running upcourt, they've already X-rayed the kid's hands and checked to see how tall he'll be."

As Ron Thomas would later write in the *San Francisco Examiner* (5/27/03), that although it wasn't common knowledge in U.S. basketball circles, Dr. James Naismith, the inventor of basketball in 1891, actually worked with missionaries who took the game to China in the 19th century.

Terry Rhoads, the Nike rep who first started working in China in 1994, points out that while basketball is only the 2nd most popular sport in China, behind soccer, it is "catching up because of two reasons; the country's compact urban environment — 14 million people live in Shanghai alone — and the NBA's exposure on television . . . Fans can watch from one to four tape-delayed games each week . . . (And)For a kid to find a soccer field in Beijing or Shanghai, it is almost impossible . . . In basketball, all you need is a ball and a rim."

Detroit Piston's scout Tony Rozzone told Murphy, "There are over 200 million registered basketball players in China." He tells of being in the Northern part of the country and finding 20 kids between the ages of 13-17 who were 7 feet tall. "You can't find five 7-footers over here in America between those ages ...And there's a 12-year-old kid over there that I worked out who's already 6'11", They're saying he might be 7'8"."

With a population of 1.3 billion, it's only

logical that China will produce a number of physically talented basketball players. Add in the government-run sports development leagues, the social emphasis on physical fitness, and the active presence of the NBA and businesses like Nike, which regularly sponsors training tournaments and builds basketball courts for the Chinese population — Yao Ming didn't look like such a risk after all.

As draft day approached, the Houston Rockets frantically tried to work out the details of Yao Ming's release from China. Several days before the draft, Xin Lancheng, the Commissioner of the Chinese Basketball Association, announced to the *People's Daily online*, "The Rockets should have confidence in selecting Yao. They should see no obstacle. The Rockets have had common understanding with us on drafting Yao."

The final sticking point, how they would compensate the Shanghai Sharks for the loss of their star player, had been worked out.

On June 27, 2002, Carroll Dawson, General Manager of the Houston Rockets, stepped to the podium at Madison Square Garden in New York and announced Yao Ming as the first international player ever chosen #1 in the NBA draft.

Through a live video feed from Shanghai, where he was preparing to play for the Chinese National Team in a series of upcoming international tournaments, Yao announced, "Houston, I am come."

The most ecstatic person of all may have been NBA Commissioner David Stern. As reported on *eastday.com*, Stern couldn't stop raving about the draft pick.

"It's a great and marvelous moment for the Rockets, for the NBA and for the whole world," Stern said. "And especially for China."

He might as well have added it was a great day for Nike, Reebok, Coke, Pepsi, Visa, Apple Computer, and any number of other U.S. businesses. Because once Yao was announced as the #1 draft pick, the marketers started to crank into high gear.

Marketing Yao Ming

Even before Yao Ming had played his first game, the international marketing campaign began.

Not that Ming was solely responsible for that. The Commissioner of the NBA, David Stern, had been working for a decade and a half to expand the audience for the NBA. Basketball is the second most popular sport globally, behind soccer, and Stern for years had been allowing tape-delayed broadcasts of NBA games to countries around the globe. Initially, those broadcast rights were dirt cheap, but as the NBA's popularity rose, so too did the rates for broadcasting rights, and income for the NBA.

When Yao had been denied the right to apply for the NBA draft a year earlier, in 2001, Stern didn't just sit around for a year and wait for Ming to become available.

Yao Ming

According to the *People's Daily online* of March 7, 2001, Mike Denzel, vice-president and general-manager of the NBA's Asia division met with Yao Songping, the deputy director of the Shanghai Sports Administration, and worked out a deal to set up an NBA marketing office in Shanghai, and another in Beijing.

Nike, Reebok, and other sporting apparel makers were also steadily increasing their efforts in China. A culture of capitalist marketing was beginning to take hold.

Now that he had been drafted #1, a position that automatically generated a great deal of publicity and exposure, Yao Ming offered the NBA a major inroad into potentially the largest market on the globe. Coke, Reebok, Nike, Skybox and other companies immediately began arranging deals that would enable them to capitalize on Yao Ming's developing status as an international celebrity.

The Houston Rockets began an advertising campaign that featured Yao's image on billboards, with the slogan 'This Could be the Start of Something Big'. They produced a Yao

Gentle Giant of Basketball

bobble-head doll that was two inches taller than any of the other players' dolls.

Even China got in on the act. Before Yao signed his contract with Houston, Chinese beer maker Yanjing signed a contract with the Rockets.

Businesses looked at Yao as a two-way street. He could open Chinese markets for Western companies, and open Western markets for the Chinese. In the U.S., he offered a way to pitch products to the large number of Chinese-Americans living in this country.

Television executives were similarly thrilled. After Yao was drafted, eight regional Chinese television carriers signed on for the right to broadcast Houston games in China. Before the season was over, four more regional Chinese carriers would sign contracts, making that an even dozen new carriers who would be paying six figure fees to the NBA for the right to broadcast a small number of NBA games to their Chinese consumers.

In North America, every city with a large Asian population began making arrangements to

Yao Ming

The rookie acquitted himself well against his toughest matchup, the gargantuan Shaquille O'Neal of the Los Angeles Lakers. Here the Rockets won 108-104 in overtime.

purchase broadcast rights for a select number of Houston games. Blocks of tickets were being purchased in NBA cities in the U.S. and Canada for games when the Rockets would come to town.

Everyone, it seemed, stood to benefit by the fact that Yao had been drafted #1. Nike already

Gentle Giant of Basketball

owned an exclusive shoe contract with him, good for another year. Reebok held the NBA rights to Yao's jersey. Upper Deck released Yao Ming cards that were commanding $150 apiece before they were even printed. Season ticket sales to Houston games skyrocketed.

The biggest winner of all, perhaps, was China. China desperately wanted to host the 2008 Olympic games. A number of countries were balking at that prospect because of the well-documented human rights abuses perpetrated by the Chinese government.

But the power of money trumped the moral concerns about granting an Olympic venue to China.

No one admits there was a *quid prop quo*, an actual deal. But the details of Yao Ming's contract with the Houston Rockets were worked out just about the same time as the Chinese government was awarded the rights to host the 2008 Olympics.

The prospect of Yao Ming becoming a world-class international media figure, and thus leading the world to China for the 2008 Olympics, left marketers salivating.

Texas officials were pleased, too, with the notion that the city of Houston, which planned to make a serious bid to host the 2012 Olympics, could count on Yao to enhance their stature as an international city.

There was only one question, it seemed, left to be answered. A question that occasionally got overlooked in all the hoopla over the 'selling' of Yao Ming.

Could the kid play basketball well enough to make a career out of the NBA?

Or was he destined to be just another bust?

First Taste

Players on NBA teams are supposed to work out, under team supervision, in the off-season so that by the time training camp begins, usually in late August, they'll already be in top physical condition, and so can focus on learning their team's offensive and defensive plays.

Success in the regular season is dependent, to a large extent, on how well the players learn to work with each other during training camp.

Yao Ming, however, was two months late to training camp. Under the terms of Houston's contract with China, Yao would not report until after China's summer tournament season had been completed. By the time Ming arrived in Houston, there were only two weeks left before the start of the 2002 season. He had missed 75% of the preseason preparation time for his NBA team.

Veteran NBA observers were curious to see,

not just if Yao could play at the NBA level, but what would be the reaction of his Rocket teammates when Yao reported late to camp.

Many young American first round draft picks drive to the arena in their $50,000 SUVs, swagger onto the court, their entourage in tow. They might mouth the proper phrases for the television cameras, but their humility is as transparent as plastic wrap. In this country, Big Attitude is seen as a plus.

Yao Ming arrived two months late to training camp riding in a car driven by his father — Yao didn't have a driver's license yet.

He did have a custom made bicycle on order, but there was little else to show he was another one of those instant millionaires made by athletic success: no gold chains, no 'posses', no outrageous designer clothing.

Yao brought with him a great sense of humility, and humor. These traits helped him to be readily accepted by his teammates. One of the big ice breakers was when he taught them how to trash talk in Chinese.

But trashtalking doesn't help on the court if

Gentle Giant of Basketball

you can't back it up. Yao's lack of practice time with his new team was apparent when the season began.

In his first game, a Rocket loss to Indiana, Yao played a total of 11 minutes. Rudy T. had said he planned to bring Yao along sowly, but still, his fans were disappointed he didn't play more. Although, even when he was on the court he wasn't effective.

He failed to score a point, grabbed only two rebounds, and picked up three fouls in eleven minutes.

It was a basketball failure; but it was a success with TV executives.

An average NBA game draws 1.1 million viewers in the United States. In China alone, Yao Ming's first game in the NBA, broadcast live to China at 8 a.m., drew 6 million viewers. An additional 6 million Chinese watched the taped replay the following night.

That's twelve million potential consumers for an advertiser's products.

In Yao's second game, against Denver, he

didn't play much better, scoring only 3 points on a 1-for-5 shooting effort.

The critics crawled out of their holes and began to proclaim him a bust.

The lack of practice time with his teammates certainly was making it difficult for Yao Ming to be effective on the court. Just as important, the extended summer tournament season with the Chinese National team had left him exhausted. He hadn't had any time off in over a year. He'd gone straight from the Shanghai Sharks to the Chinese National team to the Houston Rockets.

As he wrote in the November 8th edition of his online journal, carried on the Rocket's homepage, "I don't feel like I have rested in a while, and I feel somewhat fatigued. I feel I need more rest."

But Yao didn't dwell on his exhaustion. He ended his journal entry with a hint at his commitment. "Everyone please know that I'm working hard on getting better and learning the NBA, so hopefully you'll see the results soon."

Glimpses of Success

Although some basketball fans in the U.S. appeared ready to abandon the Yao Ming bandwagon after just two games, fans in China were much more patient with their native son. Yao's debut on his home court in Houston was slated for Saturday, November 3. The game would be broadcast live in Shanghai. Because of the time difference, it would be shown early in the morning, when people were heading to work.

Despite the early morning broadcast time, one hundred and fifty fans gathered in the ballroom of a Shanghai hotel to watch Yao's debut on a big screen televsion. The Rockets were facing the Toronto Raptors, led by superstar Vince Carter.

Carter was well-known in China. The previous summer he and Yao Ming had staged an

Yao has been instrumental in bringing a significant number of Asian fans into the basketball arena. Here is part of an enthusiastic audience at Asian American Night during a Rockets-Celtics game at Fleet Center in Boston in February, 2003.

exhibition dunk contest for children at a Shanghai arena.

Yao's fans in China cheered his every move, called out to the screen to 'Give Yao the ball' whenever he was on the court.

Ming didn't disappoint. He turned in his first respectable outing of the season, scoring 8 points, pulling down 4 rebounds, and blocking a shot.

The variety of ways he scored showed why the Rockets had been so intrigued by his talent that they drafted him #1. One basket was a hook shot, another came when he drove around his defender and put a lay-up off the glass. But for the hometown fans, the high point came in the third quarter when Yao slammed home a dunk.

"I was more relaxed tonight. I was more involved," Yao said after the game, as reported in the November 4, 2002 edition of *eastday.com*.

Houston won the game, and this time Yao could exit to the locker room knowing he had contributed to his team's victory.

Slowly, Yao got used to the NBA style of basketball. Rudy T. was determined to take it slow with his rookie, bringing him off the bench, limiting his minutes. He didn't want to put too much pressure on Ming.

In his first four games, Yao averaged only 2.5 points per contest. Then came the fifth game of the young season, the November 17 game against the Los Angeles Lakers.

Initially this was billed as a marquee

matchup between Shaquille O'Neal and Yao Ming. But Shaq was out with an injury.

Even without Shaq, the Lakers were a talented team. They were the defending world champs. The game had a playoff atmosphere for Houston.

When L.A. started 6'9" Samaki Walker at center, Rudy T. countered with Eddie Griffin. He kept Yao Ming on the bench, as was his usual pattern.

But once Yao got in, he dazzled. He scored 20 points for the first time in his NBA career, shooting a perfect 9 for 9 from the field. It was clearly the breakthrough game the Rockets had been hoping for.

Still, Rudy T. didn't want to rush Yao. He gave his rookie more minutes, but continued to hold him in reserve. In his next four games, Yao, his confidence and comfort level increasing, averaged double figures in scoring, 10 points per game. More impressively, he shot a stunning 67% from the field.

Like all rookies, Yao struggled with consistency. Some games he excelled, some games he looked overwhelmed. For the Rockets, it was heartening that his best individual performances often came against top teams.

On November 27, he scored 30 points against the first-place Dallas Mavericks. December 1st same him haul in 18 rebounds against soon-to-be league MVP center Tim Duncan and the San Antonio Spurs, the team that would eventually win the NBA championship that season. On December 16, against one of the NBA's toughest defensive teams, the Miami Heat, Yao blocked 5 shots and pulled down 8 offensive rebounds.

As Yao Ming's game heated up, so did the marketing offers. Apple Computers paid Yao big money to star in a TV commercial with Verne Troyer, the 2'8" actor best known for his role as mini-me in the Austin Powers movies. Ming inked an exclusive deal with Gatorade and was featured in a TV ad that also starred N.Y. Yankee's all-star shortstop Derek Jeter, and Pro-Bowl quarterback Peyton Manning of the Indianapolis Colts.

Then VISA signed Yao Ming to star in what

was intended to be their signature ad for the Superbowl.

Yao Ming's game was improving, he was becoming a major marketing star, ticket sales were up in Houston, and around the league when Yao played, the Chinese television broadcasts were pulling in unprecedented numbers; there was only one thing left that could enhance his visibility. If only Yao Ming could win enough votes to earn a spot on the NBA all-star team as the starting center.

All Star Controversy

In the NBA, the fans vote for the starters on the All Star team. In the Western Conference, the conference the Houston Rockets play in, the center position was strong. Tim Duncan of the San Antonio Spurs is generally considered the most talented center in the league, and one of the best to ever play the game. But he can only make the starting All Star team if he is listed on the ballot as a forward.

That's because the one player no one had come close to beating out in nine years for the starting berth at center, was Los Angeles Laker superstar, Shaquille O'Neal. Shaq, with the type of overwhelming power game only a man who weighs 360 pounds can possess, was perhaps the most dominating big man ever. Plus, Shaq played in L.A. With its huge fan base, and the nationally televised games that featured the Lakers more than any other team, there seemed no way Yao Ming could possibly earn a starting spot on the all star team.

Until the NBA stepped in.

Working out of their China offices, the NBA set up a Chinese language website so that fans in China could vote for the All Star starters. Although the fans could vote for whoever they wanted, it was clear that Yao's countrymen would vote overwhelmingly for Ming.

Was this an example of a marketing concern driving the All Star selection process? It's hard not to see it that way. The basketball games in China were regularly reaching a television audience of 15 to 16 million people, larger even than the number of people who viewed the NBA finals. The number of families with television sets in China reached 287 million — a larger number than the total U.S. population.

China was the only country where the NBA set up a website in their own language where fans could vote. There was no German language voting site, no Russian, no Spanish, only the

Gentle Giant of Basketball

English language sites, and the Chinese site.

As Yao Ming's vote totals edged closer to Shaquille O'Neal's, not everyone was happy with the attention the Chinese rookie received.

The New Racism?

Yao's online journal entry for December 10, 2003 revealed a young man adjusting to life in a foreign country. In a league where some highly visible players hung out in strip clubs or watched trash action movies, it was refreshing to hear how Yao enjoyed seeing the new Harry Potter movie, or eating at KFC.

Interestingly, he still hadn't found time to visit Houston's Chinatown.

Like many young men his age, Yao Ming spent a great deal of his free time playing computer games. A fan mag has noted that Counter-Strike is one of his favorites. But unlike most young men his age in the U.S., Yao Ming was still living with his parents.

Though he seemed to be adjusting well, not everyone in the U.S. was comfortable with the success, and attention, Yao Ming received.

For the most part, there were few angry

Gentle Giant of Basketball

taunts directed Yao's way by fans in the NBA cities where the Rockets played in what was coming to be known as the 'Yao Ming Tour'. Most of the fans were enthusiastic and supportive. Yet some of the celebrations at NBA arenas trafficked in false stereotypes that unwittingly displayed an ignorance that bordered on racial insensitivity.

The Miami Heat celebrated Yao's December 16 visit by giving fortune cookies to their fans. Fortune cookies are unknown in mainland China.

Although Yao graciously refused to criticize the minor incidents of insensitivity he came upon, deep down he must've been hurt by the harsh racism displayed by one of the NBA's premiere players — L.A. Lakers center Shaquille O'Neal.

Shortly after Houston picked Yao Ming #1 in the draft, Shaq appeared on Fox Television's "Best Damn Sports Show Period." On that show, Shaq ridiculed Ming by offering a bad imitation of Chinese speech, some fake Kung Fu moves, and a warning that he'd see how tough

Yao Ming

Yao was after Shaq smashed him in the face with an elbow.

The NBA and the U.S. media greeted Shaq's remarks with silence, although the Asian media complained.

As pointed out in *AsianWeek.com*, "Jimmy 'The Greek' Snyder, NBA Head Coach Dan Issel, and former Speaker of the U.S. House of Representatives Trent Lott... all lost their jobs due to comments offensive to Blacks or Hispanics. Golfer Fuzzy Zoeller, baseball pitcher John Rocker, and basketball star Isaiah Thomas were all forced to apologize for racially insensitive remarks."

In refusing to even acknowledge that Shaq's remarks were beyond the pale, *AsianWeek.com* argued, the U.S. media was upholding a double standard, where racism against Asians was treated as if it were acceptable. They were incensed that Shaq was not held accountable for his remarks.

As Yao Ming's All Star vote totals grew, Shaq spoke out again. On December 16, on Fox Sports Radio's "Tony Bruno Morning Extravaganza" show, Shaq, when asked about the upcoming showdown between himself and Yao Ming in the January 17 Lakers vs. Houston game said: "Tell Yao Ming, 'Ching-chong-yang-wah-ah-soh'".

AsianWeek.com was irate. "National and local (U.S.) news agencies have consciously ignored Shaq's racist comments." *AsianWeek* claimed they contacted the *Los Angeles Times*, *Sports Illustrated*, and the Associated Press, but none of those organizations was willing to cover the story.

To further the degradation of the Asian and Asian-American community, on December 17 Tony Bruno defended Shaq's remarks and then asked listeners to call in with their Chinese sports jokes.

"If a white player had . . . made monkey sounds to taunt a black player," *AsianWeek.com* wrote, "It would have been a national controversy. But . . . Chinese and Asians are fair game."

Perhaps at the core of this willingness to allow attacks on Asians was a fear that foreign-born players were taking playing slots on NBA teams away from U.S.-born players. Ex-All Star forward Charles Barkley, working as a TV analyst at the NBA draft, openly brought up this issue when he made this exact argument.

As the race for starting center grew heated, network personnel got involved in the debate. ABC sportscaster Brent Musberger, on a Christmas day broadcast, worried that "hordes" of Chinese voters might deprive Shaq of the right to start at center.

No one knows how Yao Ming felt about the racial taunting. He brushed aside questions that focused on it, and concentrated on improving his game. But everything seemed to be building to a head.

By the time the Lakers came to Houston for their January 17 game, the voting momentum appeared to be swinging Yao's way. There was a feeling that the clash of these two titans might be the deciding factor in who started for the Western Conference All Star team.

The basketball game lived up to its billing. Yao Ming was sensational in the early minutes.

Gentle Giant of Basketball

He blocked Shaq's first three shots, and made 3 out of 4 of his own shots.

Then Yao went cold. He missed his next seven shots. Shaq began to power his way to the basket again and again and again.

In a hard fought contest that seemed more like a playoff game, the Houston Rockets beat the L.A. Lakers 108-104 in overtime.

Shaq scored 31 points and pulled down 13 rebounds. Yao Ming's stat line read: 10 points, 10 rebounds, 6 blocked shots.

Shaquille O'Neal had clearly won the individual match-up, and he let people know about it.

Yao Ming focused on the important victory for his team.

If Shaq thought his dominance on the court would make fans realize he deserved to start at center over the Chinese rookie, he was wrong.

On January 24th, the final vote totals showed Yao Ming with 1.28 million votes, to beat out the 9-time all star, Shaquille O'Neal, who had garnered only 1.05 million votes. Yao Ming was also the first rookie voted into an All

Star game since Tim Duncan had been voted in in 1998.

At that point in the season, Yao was averaging 12.6 points, 7.9 rebounds and 2.03 blocks per game. These were excellent stats for a rookie. While he was obviously having an outstanding first year, it did seem the NBA decision to let people in China vote online had influenced the final outcome.

The decision seemed to have more to do with business than basketball. Marketing executives were ecstatic that Yao made the starting lineup. They anticipated a TV audience of 3.1 billion for the game, with huge numbers of them tuning in on China's close to 300 million television sets.

The All Star game was one more step in creating an international product spokesman out of this soft-spoken 22-year-old from Shanghai.

A Tired Finish

Although Yao Ming and his fans in China might have been thrilled about his outpolling Shaq in the voting for the starting center position for the Western Conference in the NBA All Star game, the other all star players might not have appreciated the way Shaq's dominance was dismissed. No one said anything about it publicly, but once the game started, Yao might as well have not even been on the court.

He played only 17 minutes in the game, which went to overtime, and during his time on the court he touched the ball only once near the hoop. He shot it in for his only 2 points of the game. His one shot attempt was the fewest by anyone on either team. To some observers, it clearly looked as if Ming's teammates were pretending he wasn't even out there.

Yao Ming

Already one of the best shot-blockers in the game, here Yao deflects a shot by Kenyon Martin (6) of the New Jersey Nets.

Gentle Giant of Basketball

Shaquille O'Neal, by contrast, took 14 shots in his 26 minutes of court time.

If it bothered Ming that, despite being voted in, he received less playing time than all but a couple of players on either team, he didn't show it. He kept a positive profile, cheering on his teammates, and spoke only about what a great honor it was for him to be at the game.

January and February had been excellent months for Yao Ming. Basketball-wise, he'd been voted to the starting All Star team, he was playing well for the Houston Rockets, who were in the hunt for a playoff berth, and he was considered to be the prime candidate to win the Rookie of the Year award.

As far as marketing went, he'd signed deals with several major companies, had been showcased in VISA's Superbowl ad, and was on track to earn $10 million in endorsement deals in this, his first year in the league.

But there's a Buddhist belief that one should never get too excited at good fortune, or too upset by misfortune. Life goes in cycles. Positives and negatives tend to balance out.

Yao Ming

By mid-March, Yao Ming was nearing the end of a string of 27 out of 29 games during which he had scored in double figures. The Houston Rockets looked like they were on the verge of beating out the Phoenix Suns, and their prize rookie Amare Stoudamire, for the 8th and final playoff spot in the Western Conference.

Then misfortune struck twice. Yao Ming hit the wall. The long season, from its start in China through the rigors of an 82 game NBA schedule, almost 3 times as long as the Chinese Basketball Association's schedule, left Yao Ming exhausted. In a span of 4 games during which the Rockets had to face Conference rivals San Antonio, Sacramento, and both Los Angeles teams, the Lakers and the Clippers, Yao Ming appeared to lose all his energy.

Through the first 62 games Yao had shot the ball at a 52% clip. During that four game stretch in March, he made only 7 of 28 shots, 25% from the field. Houston lost 3 of the 4 games. That effectively dashed any realistic hopes they had of making the playoffs.

Ming did pull it together to score double

figures in 8 of his last 10 games, but his fatigue showed in his shooting numbers. He had games where he made 3 of 9, 6 of 14, 3 of 11, and 2 of 13 shots from the field. His rebounding and blocked shots were down, too.

In the last 14 games of the season, Yao Ming averaged only 11 points per game, vs. the 14 per game clip he had been scoring at during the first 68 games. While he had been shotting at a 52% clip for most of the season, in the last 14 games he made only 39% of his shots. His shooting percentage, for the first time, dipped below .500. He finished the year making .498 percent of his shots — still an excellent figure, 3rd among rookies and 15th in the entire NBA. But it was clear he had faded at the end. And with his fade went Houston's chances of making the playoffs. The Phoenix Suns squeaked by them for the 8th and final position.

It would be unfair to blame the Houston Rocket's fade on one player, and a rookie at that. Other players on the team faded down the stretch as well. Perhaps most problematic, their popular coach, Rudy Tomjanovich, was diagnosed with bladder cancer, and had to leave the team just as they needed his experienced hand to guide them on a final playoff push. The loss of Rudy T. was the single biggest contributing factor in the Rocket's demise.

On a personal note, Yao's fade prevented him from winning the Rookie of the Year award, which went to Amare Stoudamire. For the year, Stoudamire outscored Ming 14.2 points to 13.5, and outrebounded him 8.8 to 8.2 per game. More importantly, as Yao Ming would recognize, Stoudamire's team made the playoffs. Yao Ming would have to content himself with a second place finish in the balloting.

Yao Ming's last online journal entry, dated April 22, 2003, showed a more pensive side to the rookie. He spoke about the team losing many games they should've won, yet still being only one step away from the playoffs. He spoke of the loss of the coach as being the biggest reason the team faded. He understood there were adjustments he needed to make to the NBA, and his team. "The weakest point of our team is not any position, but learning to play together. The team took a while getting used to me and it was an adjustment for me to get used to them." Instead of pointing a finger at others, he brought it back to his own responsibility. "Because I like to pass the ball a lot, I need to know what position they like to be when they shoot, and what circumstance they feel more comfortable in. So I need to know their differences and that takes time to learn."

He also told his fans that he would rest for a while but he would be playing for the Chinese National team. "Playing for the national team is an honor."

Perhaps remembering the step-by-step progress made by a younger Yao Ming and his CBA team, the Shanghai Sharks, Ming spoke of being positive the Rockets would make the playoffs in 2003-2004. "If everyone could be in the arena rooting for us," he wrote, "I think we will not let you down next year."

But is there life outside of basketball for Yao Ming? It would be hard not to call him well-rounded, given that so much of his life has been on the court. He swims when he can, and utilizes weightlifting. Shanghai-style chicken soup, followed by chocolate ice cream, is reported to be his favorite meal, though he is known to count on steamed dumplings, also with soup, for a pre-game boost. His favorite car is a Mercedes-Benz. Almost certainly, he is kept too busy to have a full-time girl friend, though he is certain to start appearing soon on most-eligible-bachelor lists.

Yao seems to be a *nice* young man, so unlike a number of current gangster-type stars in different sports. One evidence of this came on Sunday, May 11th, when the National Basketball Association's 24-hour television network, NBA TV, helped to produce a special telethon with Shanghai's Great Sports Channel. The show was a benefit to raise money to find a cure for the flu-like disease SARS, which so far has been most prevalent in Hong King and mainland China, killing some 240 people while at one point causing such widespread fear that whole cities were shut down, the streets deserted, the shops and stores shuttered and locked.

A special guest, and the reason most people

tuned in, was Yao Ming, who made a short speech. Donations, which reached about $300,000 for the event, doubled while Yao was on the screen. A small army of current and former NBA players also were in force during the show, including Commissioner David Stern. Former NBA great Magic Johnson made an appearance by satellite, as did Shaq O'Neal, who took the opportunity to mend fences with the Asian community and even memorized several Chinese phrases for use during his appearance.

The telethon was the first ever from mainland China. It is a measure of the respect and love with which Yao Ming already is held in both countries, that he was guest of honor. Over the next few years, if his talent and his personality hold up, this unassuming young man has a chance to become a truly important person, an international Ambassador of Sport, the start of a new tying-together of commerce and popular culture, of East and West.

Bibliography

INTERNET SITES

www.AsianWeek.com, unspecified dates, 2002, 2003

Eastday.com 2/09/03, 6/27/02, 10/21/02, 11/04/02, 12/21/02

ESPNMAG.com, 12/25/00, May 2002, 6/21/02, 7/25/02

China Daily online, July 25, 2002

www.examiner.com, 5/27/03

www.globe.com, 2/25/03

HoustonChronicle.com, 6/21/02, 6/22/02, 6/25/02, 8/16/02, 3/31/03, 4/02/03, 5/26/03

www.NBA.com, unspecified dates, 2002, 2003

www.philstar.com, unspecified dates 2003

www.sports.sohu.com, 2/02/03, 2/25/03

www.TIME.com 5/11/01, 2/10/03

www.TIMEasia.com, 9/20/99

www.usatoday.com, 1/23/03, unspecified dates 2002, 2003

www.washingtonpost.com, 12/13/02
www.wcymoresports.thestar.com, 11/02/02
www.yaoming.net, unspecified dates 2003
www.yaomingmania.com, 5/26/03, unspecified dates, 2002, 2003

INTERNET CITATIONS

Associated Press, 3/28/03, unspecified dates 2002, 2003
People's Daily online, 3/16/01, 3/19/01, 9/01/01, 6/27/02, 9/11/02, 9/25/02, 10/06/02, 12/30/02
Reuters News Service, 8/30/01, unspecified dates 2003
Sports Illustrated online, unspecified dates 2002
SI for Kids online, unspecified dates 1996
Xinhua News Agency, 8/31/01, 7/03/02, 10/15/02

NEWSPAPERS

San Francisco Examiner, May 27, 2003
Chicago Tribune, Feb. 7, 2003

Index

Bateer, Menk 26, 35, 38

Barkley, Charles 92

Baxter, Lonnie 50

Carter, Vince 39, 79

Cayne, Michael 45, 65

Daniels, Lloyd 'Sweetpea' 52

Di, Fang Geng 11-14

Dixon, Juan 50

Duffy, Frank 31, 45

Duncan, Tim 83, 85 , 94

Falk, David 45

Harris, Del 27

Jeter, Derek 83

Jordan, Michael 30, 62-63

Manning, Peyton 83

Musberger, Brent 92

Olajuwon, Hakeem 18-20, 24, 56, 63

O'Neill, Shaquille 72. 82, 85, 87, 89-93, 95, 97, 103

Payton, Gary 39

Rhoads, Terry 8, 10, 30, 66

Sabonis, Arvydas 22-27

Stern, David 45, 68-69, 103

Stoudamire, Amare 98, 100

Tomjanovich, Rudy 56, 77, 81-82, 99-100

Yuan, Yao Zhi 11-14

Zhi, Wang Zhi 26, 35, 37-38, 53 57-58

About the Author

RICHARD KRAWIEC is the author of the well-received novels *Time Sharing* and *Faith in What?* as well as a book of short stories, *Fools of God*. His previous sports biography is *Sudden Champion: The Sarah Hughes Story*. He lives in Raleigh, North Carolina with his family.